LEFT HANDED THROUGH TIME

LEFT HANDED THROUGH TIME

John H. Baldwin

Cork Hill Press
Carmel

CORK HILL PRESS™

Cork Hill Press
597 Industrial Drive, Suite 110
Carmel, IN 46032-4207
1-866-688-BOOK
www.corkhillpress.com

Trade Paperback Edition: 1-59408-067-4

1 3 5 7 9 10 8 6 4 2

This book is dedicated to the person
who provided the fulcrum upon
which I was able to lever the good things in my life.
Always supportive, never ready to interfere,
always forgiving of my faults,
never willing to take any credit for my successes…
John Anderson

CONTENTS

Chapter 1

What Was Then - A Thirty-Two Year Marriage

Chapter 2

Through the Singles - the Search

Chapter 3
Found – Josephine

Chapter 4
Love and Romance

Chapter 5
Look and See

Chapter 6
Just to Entertain

Chapter 7
Have a Thought

Chapter 8
Introspection

Chapter 9
Stories

CHAPTER 1

What Was Then – A Thirty-Two Year Marriage

SHE'S THESE

She's the Queen of all my Kingdom,
The Empress of my whole domain,
The cook, the tailor, and scullery maid,
The General of our life's campaign.

She's the mistress of my castle,
Though humble it may be,
She's my terrible tyrant and whipping boy
She's all these things to me.

So after a day of working,
Or with the coming of night,
I return to this witch or angel,
This woman I call my wife.

No other direction I'd rather go,
No place I'd rather be,
Than that wonderful castle or hovel
Where my sweet wife waits for me.

A PROPOSAL

Day to day, I wait for you;
My heart seems not to beat,
Only you can fill this void
You're my love, my life complete.

When you're gone away from me,
I exist in a world apart,
And though I walk and talk the same,
I'm a man without a heart.

You cannot question my feelings,
I've shown them a thousand ways,
There's no mistaking them either,
They're the signs that love displays.

So, sweetheart, say that you love me,
That you'll be the light in my life;
Say that you care for no other,
Say that you'll be my wife.

THE ONE-TIME SAILOR

My heart was a vessel sailing
On a sea tossed with discontent,
In search of a sheltering harbor
'Til lifes storms at last were spent

I found my haven of safety,
An island with rainbows and sun,
I struck my colors and scuttled my ship,
My sailing days were done.

But the Sea of Love's not a smooth one,
As all who have sailed it know.
Those tides that brought us together
Must ebb, as well as flow.

Take care, my love, not to wander
Too far from this beautiful shore,
Lest the winds of Fate drive you away,
And I can sail no more.

OVERDONE

Too much tinsel, too many ornaments,
Just enough balls—times three.
It's fake I know, but to me it seems
You should be able to see the tree.

A cardboard cutout, and a golden bell
An angel and a sequined star
A stegosaurus and a music sheet
A stuffed elf and a plastic car.

Gaudied up with a thousand lights
I think that's twenty strings,
No real live tree could ever hold
The weight of all these things.

She always spent those many hours
And laid each piece just there.
With boxes and boxes of tinsel
Each separate strand placed with care.

But the effect of all of this hoorah
You'd expect to be surreal
But you'd be surprised that's not the case,
It's a serenity you feel.

Oh yes it's overdone
Too much by any measure
But overdone with too much love
Makes our holiday tree a treasure.

WHAT'S LEFT FROM THIS

After thirty years she knew my weakness
And she felt so sorry for me
She worried about my health
And my lack of social life

She told me to pay the bills
As they came in, like she did
"Then you won't forget them
And balance the checkbook every month.

I know you'll cook for company
But watch your diet for balance
Not just steak, or just beans
Make yourself healthy meals.

You've got to go out you know
You can't sit in front of the TV.
Not every night.
You must not be a couch potato."

She would look at me with sad eyes
And wish that she could do more for me
She held my hand and comforted me
So sad for my unhappiness

As time went by
She could not attend me like she did
She did not love me less
There was less of her to give

We went to places we had been
With warm sand and blue water
Or crystal ice
On trout streams

The dusty streets of Mazatlan
Chicken salad and iced tea
Mexican musicians playing
Their music, just for us.

We again had sultry nights
With the car top down
Her hair kinky-curly
In the moist night air

Cherry blossoms in Washington
Marching bands in the hot afternoon
And too many cold old fashions
In the cool dim light of a capitol bar

Drinking gimlets in fine glassware
While sweaty and grimy and hopeful
As we dig and pan the muck
For California gold

The grandeur of Niagara falls
The spray cool against our skin
The grand Grand Canyon
And it's splendid color

We recalled them all together
We had the time it seemed
But she would bring me back...
"You must not be a couch potato."

And then she left me...
And had me keep the memories
Of all the good times
That need not be forgotten.

And the bad times
She had filled with good
And lectured me on living
Until I understood

She wasn't to be a loving anchor
To hold me as we were
But wanted me as happy
As what I'd been with her.

But I have my memories
Of her gentleness and caring
Of her sadness at our parting
Of our many years of sharing

And that is,
What's left for me.

THE PAST

By now the words won't burn me
I'll let go what I cannot grasp,
Her color and her gentle humor
That now only exist in the past

This lovely girl has left me,
And my memories are sweet and they last...
Of her color and her gentle humor
That now only exists in the past.

She was sweetness and caring and patient,
And I hold these memories fast...
Of her color and her gentle humor
That now only exist in the past.

And now these words don't burn me
I've let go what I cannot grasp.
I'll remember her color and humor...
But I cannot exist in the past.

SEASONS

Rambunctious spring,
With beauty all about.
Lent itself to my passions...
Passions wasted, but devout

At last, the serenity of summer
To spend at leisure pace
To test the breadths and depths of feeling
With love's comfort and embrace.

The sweetness of the season
So rich, so full of time to spend
With my life and love together
Till the year comes to an end.

An early frost has come upon us.
Too powerful, and much too soon
Now I'm bereft of comfort
Beneath this early autumn moon.

But my year is not yet gone,
And still my passions glow
I still yearn for warmth and caring
Before the coming of the snow.

I now exist for Indian summer.
That short and sweet respite
While I still care and feel and love
Before the winters chilly night

The warmth of the Indian summer
I begrudge each passing day
Without a kindred soul to share
The wonders of the way.

The passing days seem rushing
I seek, and my heart yearns
For a kindred soul to share my way
Before the weather turns.

CHAPTER 2

Through the Singles - Searching

I HOPE THE GIFT IS IN THE GIVING

Tired and beaten
The dummy made his way
Unspeaking, unfeeling
Through his humdrum day.
No plans, no pleasures
Nothing to arrange,
Today's the same as yesterday
Never any change.

So she said "hello" to him
Expecting no reply.
To pierce his silent world
She thought at least to try.
"How are you, the weathers nice
What's new for you today?"
She pried and pushed and prodded
To find a word that he could say.

Daily repetition..."And how are you?
It's as windy as can be,
I have a cold, I like your tie
My son's gone north to ski.

Do you like cake? My car won't start.
My two cats had a fight.
Taken your vacation yet?
Did you see the moon last night?"

And then a change…He spoke to her
The words don't mean a thing
But a dummy spoke, a major change
That a tender heart could bring.
And he asked her of her home life
And of the people that she knew,
And he told her of his lack of life
And what he didn't do.

Then with kind coercion
She sought to teach him how to live.
To go on drives, to meet with friends
She had a life to give.
She shared with him her friends
Showed him places that she stayed,
Showed the world was out there
To enjoy, not to evade.

She revived his flaccid spirit
Rekindled his life's flame,
Engaged his mind in living
Now nothing was the same.
The dummy smiled and said hello
His step and manner spry.
Not like the dummy of before
That seemed to wait to die.

She danced with him and held him close
While new music played,
Reintroduced life's rhythms
That his memory had betrayed.
And she sang for him sweet lyrics
That he would want to hear.
Reviving tempos long forgot
While she held him near.

Now time has passed, and we can see
As the dummy makes his way,
With the comings and the going
And the doing of his day.
He thinks of her and he cares for her
But changed, it's not the same.
For though he thinks and cares for her
He just can't say her name.

And what of her, does she want more
From the dummy she awoke?
That she invested self and soul for
A heart given to be broke?
That she awaits with patience
And a heart that needs to mend.
For a dummy who can't say her name
And can't be just a friend.

At last she's found another
This loving tender heart,
To shower her attention
To love and never part,
And have her self and soul
Set afire once again,
By a fellow who deserves her
And… Can say her name.

THE MAGIC FLOWER.

There is magic.
It's not rare or good or bad.
Yet there,
Till it is gone...
It leaves no proof, no vestige,
Of what, or why, it was...

- - -

I found a flower on my way.
So beautiful, so rare that I was taken—entranced.
Its form and color, and its fragrance—captivating.
I touched the lovely petals,
        Softly resilient, touching back.
And its fragrance filled me,
        A tropic feast of sweet coconut...
It filled my soul, and I was more than me.

I would take it with me, not pick, not harvest,
But engender its roots in me that I could
Shelter and protect and have it close...
I find a taproot so strong and deep into the past
That this blossom cannot be moved—lest it wither.
So I would stay.

I am awakened from the serenity of my trance,
Surprised at blood, a minor wound,
But blood, real and red, I nurse my finger,
And wonder how I missed the thorn before.

I attend the flower…
It's changed, still beautiful,
But it now seems to be of teak,
A lustrous rich red-brown polished glow,
Carved with loving hand to exquisite form
Its beauty more abstract, not touching back,
But for me intact.

When did my teak flower turn to brass?
Not carved but cast, in metal,
Still beautiful in form
Yet I cannot fool myself with brass
Like I could with teak.
The warmth is only mine
The blossom is cold to touch.

A patina forms.
A mist upon the metal, it's not benign but caustic.
When I touch, it burns me, it saps my soul.
Like salt upon a slug, I writhe in that same agony.
Becoming less and less and less.
If I do not escape I die, or else, no more be me.

Oh metal flower
I recollect the color, and the softness,
And the sweet tropical pheromone,
Before the metamorphosis.
Yet as you are, you're safe.
Safe from crude bumbling hands
Of those who do not understand
What you need safety from.
And you are safe, within your metal shell.
Safe from harm, safe from hurt,
Safe from care… safe from caring.

- - -

There is magic.
It's not rare or good or bad.
It was there,
But it is gone…
I have no proof, there is no sign,
Of what, or why, it was, it's gone.

But for the haunting mental trace…
Of sweet coconut.

LIKE EMC2

I have a hunger
        That you can satisfy.
I have a thirst
        That you can slack.
I am cold and
        You can make me warm.

Like a glorious sunset
        Is gone with the night
Its beauty is gone forever
        There is no time.
It was there as surely
        As a black hole in space.
But, like that black hole
        Whose mass approaches infinity,

        It has… no time.
        Nor do we.

O POSITIVE AM I

There's a name for it, I know
And a place as well, I'm sure
Where this malady of mine
Would be somewhat less obscure

Where my special weakness
Would be considered strength
Where my feelings would be measured
By their depth and not their length

Where I could be at rest
And have no fear to pain
To test untasted flavors
Till I was home again

O positive am I, I'll find
A match that's right for me
That I will find acceptance for
That heart that's meant for me

That I might match for others
O positive am I
For I'm a universal donor
Yet for myself I try

To find the match of mine for me
Not a match for them
To have the heart that I need
And need not search again

But I seek and hurt and seek
O positive am I
I need a universal donor
Like I had in time gone by

DIFFERENCES

In various discussion groups
Of difference much is made
Between the women and the men
And how that difference is displayed.

Now I'm not speaking out in general
I just repeat the lines
I've heard in groups so often
That a subgroup self defines.

The men they are insensitive
Unable to connect
Ruled by raging hormones
And lacking in respect.

The men they don't communicate
They never call you back
A fund of broken promise
Untrustworthiness a fact.

And the women who will gouge you
Take advantage to the max
Who'll have you jumping through the hoops
Never willing to relax.

Who will show you like a pony
With a halter on his nose
And try and make you someone else
A prize pup that she shows.

She doesn't really care
How this process makes you feel
To complain is being rigid
And balking's not genteel.

The folks that make these statements
In their ruts so deep it shows
Continue their complaining
Then all about them knows.

The irreconcilable difference
That they have found again
Is that women will be women
And men insist on being men.

And until some future date
When they can change their view
And lose these generalities
There will be… nothing new.

TIPS ON DATING

First and foremost you must make
Some rules that you must follow
To get and keep the upper hand
Tell the things that you'll allow.

Never let them know you're interest
Always try and act blase'
Postpone the date to meet you
Make them wait another day.

If the time to meet is seven
Never show till seven ten
It will increase anticipation
And improve your worth to them.

When choosing from the menu
The things you like ignore
Get the most expensive
Show your class for sure.

Talk about your foreign trips
Quadruple A hotels
Criticize broken English
And the pungent seaside smells.

Don't enjoy the movie
Unless it's foreign made
Subtitled is by far the best
Your good taste then displayed.

And when the night is over
Say tersely there and then
That you need your beauty sleep
You'll be seeing them again.

Now follow my directions
This plan will work you'll see
And if by chance it doesn't
Phone in a call to me.

For I am sure to be there
Waiting all alone
Hoping for a friend to call
By my telephone.

WORDS

I tell you words are cheap
And they alone prove naught
They can not serve in place of deeds
Or suffice where action's sought.

A poet has his words displayed
Laid out for all to see
With careful emotive phrasing
As a tender thought should be.

How sensitive must be his soul
To have penned that thoughtful line
How soulful is his thinking
To have that idea come to mind.

- - -

Charley sits there all alone
Janet's gone, says he's for the birds.
She says he was insensitive…
It's just he had no words.

But he loved and was attentive
Her wish was his command
But he didn't have the sweet words
To thrill and win her hand.

So he's alone and she's alone
Hearts empty, unfulfilled
For the lack of flowery phrases
A sweet liaison is killed.

He shouldn't have to say it
His manners proved his place
Caring, not his verbal sharing
Should have proved his case…

- - -

Now Andy writes with feeling
Romance and ideas flow
Ensconced with his tender feelings
Imprisoned, and on death row.

I tell you words are cheap
And sensitivities not a rhyme
To confuse just words with feeling
Is an intellectual crime.

FIFTY FIFTY

It was the perfect situation
The marriage of the pair
They had enlightened reason
And a life to share.

They both had education
Jobs that were well paid
Each knew how to keep a home
And the game plan to be played.

Fifty fifty was the deal
On this they both agreed
They would share and share alike
Thus fulfilling every need.

But here they sit astounded
In the counselors waiting room
Tight lipped enraged together
And they sense impending doom.

For now they know it doesn't work
To measure what half you'll give
And accept your partners meting
For this is how you live.

It's impossible to measure
Fifty fifty down the line
How can I give her her due
And not keep track of mine.

So it boiled down to scoring
Seeing who did what and when
And doing less than I did before
To even the score again

With less and less invested
Their funds of life went dry
And left the couple wondering
What went wrong and why.

Mathematics doesn't work in life
Too abstract and so unfeeling
Parsing out one's actions
To the heart is not appealing.

If you take yours and she takes hers
Little pieces lost it's clear
What was whole and healthy
Begins to disappear.

But should you insist on mathematics
There's a ratio to use
To mete your lovers needs
That's impossible to abuse.

That's a hundred and a hundred
Not one centile less
And never count what's going out
Don't even try to guess.

Just appreciate what's coming in
Recount each act that's done
And count it as a favor
And return it two for one.

Then you will find your soulmate
So pleased with you that then
All this useless counting stops
And two are one again.

It's like multiplying fractions
Unless they're more than one
There's less and less to divvy up
When the counting's done

So it's a hundred and a hundred
Don't settle for anything less
It's the algorithm that guarantees
Your share of happiness.

CHAPTER 3

What's Now - Josephine

GRAFTING

Is this the woman
Who will define in me…
A place,
A void?
Where now exists
A just barely useful
Pumping device.
And after creating
This place,
This vacuum…
Will fill it with herself.
And then I won't be me
But we.
So much more
Than what I was before…
The grafting of our souls.

FALSE LABEL

I am chagrined to find
I have a transitory nature.
Not by choice, by treatment.
I think of old oak and weathered stone
But, it is as a breeze
I think I'm known.

A breeze is not my choice
Is not my vision
Of what I think should be.
I think of heavy antique tables
Thick walled marble urns.
Yet I'm viewed as a rippling wave
On a tide that turns.

A wave that is
And just as surely disappears
Is not the reality of me.
I think of old tomes
Leather bound with gilded pages.
Yet I am treated like a fancied cloud
With artful edges.

I do not disdain
The pleasure of a soft breeze,
A curling wave, a cloud in sunset.
But I want more than pleasures
That are too quickly passed.
I want substance, and permanence
And feelings that will last.

And passion
That fills to overflow,
Is not the reality I seek.
I do seek full possession
Of you, and all your heart.
If this can't be, please,
Make me see…
For I would rather part.

TOO QUICK?

There was a man who wandered
Who seemed to have no home
Never finding any comfort
Seeming doomed to always roam

Then one day he stopped
And no one could explain
How he could choose so quickly
The place where he'd remain.

But he really didn't wander
Though that is what it seemed
He was seeking something special
A vision that he'd dreamed.

So his stopping wasn't sudden
It took time for him you see
To find that place envisioned
Where he would want to be.

So you can't tell from where you are
The speeds that things take place
Their hidden modes and meanings
And their timings you can't trace.

So if you can permit a pace

That you can't comprehend
You'll find the sudden start
Need never have an end.

What was quick for you
For him was measured
The timing's off
But the finding treasured.

USING INTELLIGENCE

I like to consider that
I can choose
That my choices are legitimized
With the light of logic
And are free of whimsy

Yet this major decision
Fails any test
In retrospect
To prove this theory.

I don't rescind my options
I'm so pleased with what I have
But I can find no logic
That would put me where I am.

In the act of searching
There's logic to the search
But I can find no logic
That would support my find.

I was distracted by a look
Studied casual, squeaky clean
But I can find no logic
That would be swayed by that.

And yet, in my pursuit
I find a warmth and caring
That could not show before
Yet I AM in pursuit

Blind luck and good luck
And not cerebral work
Make me pleased
And glad to be.

But I will find a hidden clue
That channeled my intent
That guided my decision
And proves that I did think

And I will revel you with reasons
And have proof support my claim
That intellect was working
When my choice was made.

REVELATION

In another poem
I spoke about a choice
Spoke about a choosing
Where logic had no voice

Now I deal in retrospect
Maybe feeling usurps fact
But here is how I recollect
That most important act.

Studied casual, squeaky clean
In the milling singles crowd
All alone with head held high
Refusing to be cowed.

Bravely out there little girl
Where she didn't want to be
But bravely, even brazen
She would see what she could see.

Damn, a fellow soon approaches
He bids her welcome there
She smiles that brilliant smile
Whose warmth they both will share

No, she doesn't come here often
It's her first time to attend
It's pretty far for her to drive
But she might come back again

They chat a few more moments
The weather and the news
He receives her full attention
Now, may she be excused?

She makes her way to the ladies room
But she will not reappear
She'll be gone by another door
She'll just disappear

Another night there's dancing
I see her on the floor
I weave my way through dancers
But she is there no more

It's early and she is gone
This elusive dark haired girl
Who comes and goes like a spirit
In this curious singles whirl

If she should ever appear again
Self promises I make
I will act more sure and swiftly
Before she makes her break

I will speak to her, be first.
Ask she not go home so soon
Plead for an evening's dancing
Before she leaves the room

Studied casual squeaky clean
That luxuriant radiant smile
The kindness of full attention
Lady come, and stay a while

She came, I saw, she conquered
She was all that I saw from afar
Now I don't want things to be different
I want things to stay as they are.

If there is no evidence of logic
In the way things went at the start
There is logic in keeping things as they are
And her very close to my heart.

THE MONSTER

I have met the brown-eyed menace
Face to face.
My will removed
By the liquid brown embrace.
Powerless,
I stand here mesmerized.
Commanded,
By the power of the eyes.

So deceptive
Is the creature's smile
White teeth
That sparkle
And beguile.
They lure you to the lips
And then,
Never set you free again.

My gaze directed
By those
Graceful hands
As surely as
With iron bands.
I look into those eyes
And lose
Any power to refuse.

Arms
That gently do enfold
Belie
The anaconda hold.
Gentleness
It hides the feel
Of power
As in coils of steel.

In the tangle
Of its medusa hair
Its strands
My fingers they ensnare.
I am lost.
There is no breaking free
Her sweet venom
Overpowers me.

TIME WARP

Calibrated to a nanosecond
The time is measured thus.
On the Greenwich meridian
And is given so to us.

So there is no variation
Each successive second equal
To the one that came before it
I know this fact and still…

When the days or hours are passing
A fault there seems to be.
Some are long, some are short
Widely variant for me.

I've heard that time collapses
In the black holes out in space.
That mass destroys the clock
That measures in that place.

So there's precedence existing
For the phenomena I face.
For the arbitrary clocking
And my perceptual pace.

Something massive must exist
And though invisible I feel
It warps the time around me
And that difference is real.

When you are gone away from me
The time drags slowly by.
When you're near, the other phase,
A day in a blinking eye.

So I can choose the cadence
The tempo for my life to be.
To have that… rapid heart beat
And have you close to me.

THE SUN GOD

As I lay on the grass
Hoping only to relax
The sun shined down upon me
Through my eyelids
Giving my inner world
A soft red glow

As I lay there
Hoping only to relax
The sun shined down upon me
It made me warm
When I did not know
That I was cold

My head cradled on my hands
I now face the sun
I am relaxed With a comfort
I had known In some previous life
I am basking in its glow

I feel that I will follow
This luxurious sun
As it tracks through time
Like flowers Of the field
In phototropic loyalty

Like a tropical reptile
I need the sun
Though I bask and enjoy
I require its warmth
So that I can move
So I can breathe
I can live

Like the Aztec
I now worship This sun
And like the Aztec
I see the need
Of human sacrifice
I provide a living heart
As proof of my fidelity

GOOD MORNING

Sleepy eyes that smile,
Could any thing be sweeter
Than that under covers warmth
For the one who's here to greet her.

Sleepy eyes that smile and more
Implying words unsaid
Mixing tenderness and passion
For the one who shares her bed.

Sleepy eyes that offer
An embrace with warmth I know
A last few precious moments
Before I have to go.

Sleepy eyes that say goodbye
Parting sadness oh so slight
Consoled with the awareness
I'll return to her tonight.

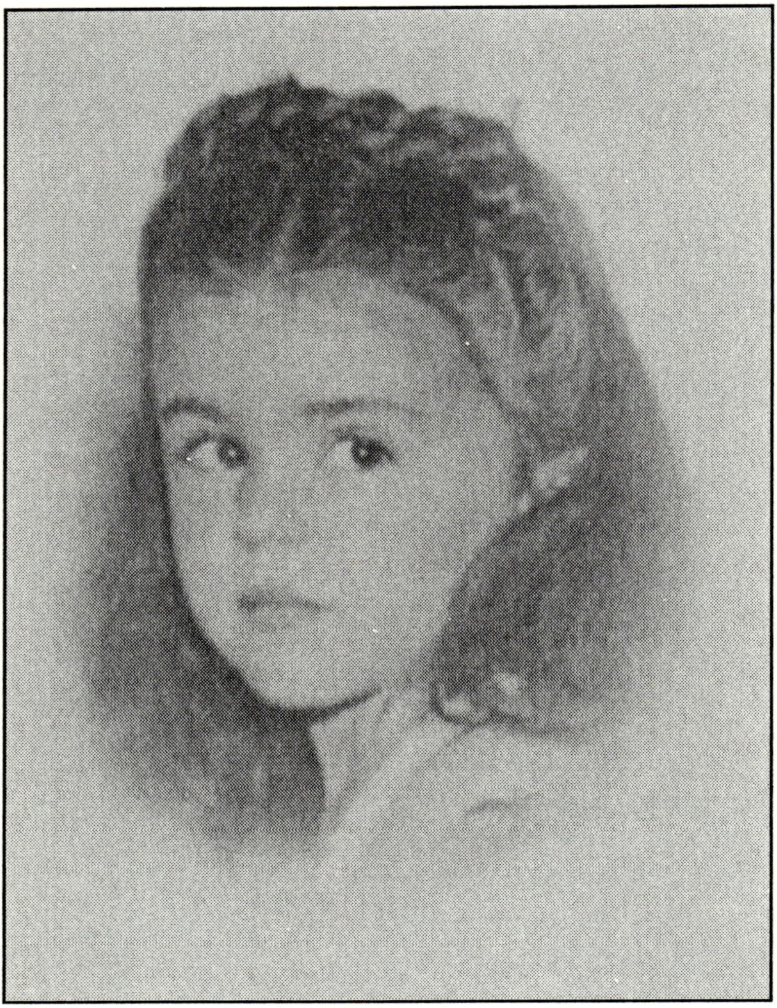

THE YOUNG GIRL POSING

A stray wisp of hair above the arching brow
A rebellious hint, it's not so different now.
The dark eyes looking back
Querying the expectation
Of why the pose
Should be so studied and exact.
Perhaps that's why
The sweetly shaped young lips
Don't smile.

They are not pursed in petulance
You can see the smile will be there.
But will she smile falsely?
The jaw line tells you no...
She will smile when she chooses,
And her smile will be pleasing,
As it is now.

Half a century has not hidden
The beautiful child.
You can see her sweetness,
And her innocence, and her lack of guile,
When she chooses...
And she shares her smile.

THE INSTRUMENT

I started, and the notes were often sour,
Too abrupt, with timing never smooth
But I found that time and patience
Made the sound improve.

Dutifully I strummed,
Where I could make the cord,
But only strident tones
Were given as reward.

This labor wasn't wasted
As I have come to find
For the logic of my effort
Showed the workings of my mind.

But the music wasn't music
It was sounds that were related
Missing some unknown measure
Lack of feeling demonstrated.

Over time this changed
As we grew to know our place
The tempos grew concordant
And feeling set the pace.

Then the music flowed
Time filled with melody
The instrument I played
Became a part of me.

I began to feel, unthinking.
Softly touch the strings, caress.
I heard the wordless lyrics
That the mind can only guess.

And as this instrument came to be
Not just a thing apart
It plays for me, the music
That I hear within my heart.

WHAT HAPPENED?

Did you fall, or were you pushed,
When did it occur?
Is there a progression
From which we may infer?

Was it an option that you chose,
Or was it just by chance?
A calculated risk,
Or a flier on romance?

Did you choose to go this far
Or are you now surprised
To find your heart upon your sleeve
Before you realized.

It really doesn't matter
How this came to pass
Just what route you took
To be with me at last.

What matters is, that your are here
A place you want to be
A place existing nowhere else
A place to be with me.

So if it was an accident
Or if it was a shove
Or an arithmetic choice
Or any choice above

I will think surrender
As a major function of
The miracle that I enjoy
The gift I have… your love.

SELF SATISFIED

He's so smug, with what he has
He can see no fault at all
Displaying blind assurance
And unmitigated gall.

He really doesn't understand
The fineness of the line
That separate the feelings
Heart broken and sublime.

Doesn't he care of others
Who thought their risk was slight
They thought they had it all
But they sleep alone tonight.

Thoughts like this are foreign
He doesn't choose to hear
Of jeopardy he courts
Without an ounce of fear

But he will get what he deserves
For arrogance and pride
His rightful comeuppance
That will not be denied

He will get the loyalty
And he will get the caring
And he will get the piece of mind
That comes from total sharing

And he, because of no reserve
No room for seeds of doubt
Has egoistic arrogance
His smugness seems to shout

I have it all, I have it all
I am so pleased you see
I can take for granted
That she is here with me.

I have no need to worry,
Or have a need to care
Whatever kismet brings me
I know that she'll be there.

So I have no need of future
My present lasts past then
So I'll be smug in the here and now
Till never comes back again.

POINTS

There are points of separation
That I have come to find
Which make me feel uneasy
And prey upon my mind.

I am so accustomed
To a perfect harmony
That a minor dissidence
Is troubling to me.

I know this shouldn't happen
Not the fact, the feel
And I sense a separation
That's more perceived than real.

So the infinitesimal rift
That really shouldn't count
Becomes a worry to me
A fault I must surmount.

I must trust your caring
The fact that you'll forgive
Understand the gravity
On this world in which we live.

For it will always be there
To hold us here secure
A holding, tying, binding force
That will make our world endure.

CHAPTER 4

Love and Romance

LOVE IS

Love is a look into the eyes of a smiling child.
Love is two old people sitting comfortably, not talking.
Love is pride in the accomplishments of someone else.
Love is sparkling wine and a friendly laugh,
    Hands across the table, fingers intertwined.
Love has long black hair, Is satin bosomed with full hips,
    Lowered eyes, and moistened lips.
Love is a cool hand on a fevered brow.
Love is two friends arguing.
Love is a man holding the baby gently.
Love is a woman gazing at the mountain.
Love is letting go… if need be.

BLIND MAN

Street girl, street girl
That's whispered by my friends.
They don't realize love can live,
Past the point where reason ends.

They don't know what they do to me
That I've heard these things before,
Each tale they tell makes fresh the wound,
Yet I couldn't love her more.

Don't help me if you care for me,
Though you think that I am blind,
What's important is that I be hers,
And not that she be mine.

Don't pity this poor blind man,
My ignorance is bliss.
I see nothing else but beauty
In the warmth of a street girl's kiss.

NIGHT TRAIN

I hear the night train's whistle
That lonesome, mournful sound
It seems it only sounds that way
Since you've not been around.

When I played around on you
I didn't use my head
I thought the play was just for fun
But I lost my love instead.

Now I'm so lonesome for you
I ain't never been so sad
I knew I'd miss you, honey
But I never thought so bad.

Please look my way just one more time
With that sparkle in your eye
And I won't do you wrong again
Not 'till the day I die.

Please, take me back, I'm begging
Please take me back, and then
That lonesome night train's whistle
Will be a lullaby again.

THE LETTER

Your letter came, and it's been read
A dozen times, or more.
And if I read what's written down,
It's all been said before.

"You love me, you miss me,
You wish that I were here,"
They're written here in ink, I see,
So plain... yet not so clear.

You didn't speak of what we'll do
When I get home again,
Your letter made me feel as though
I'm just a casual friend.

Your written words are much the same
As you wrote me other times,
But important parts you're leaving out—
Those parts between the lines.

Perhaps, I've been away too long,
Your heart has changed its mind,
If this is so, please write in ink,
Not in between the lines.

SEX

Sex is about in all sizes,
With various shapes, and directions
So it's incumbent on me
To just let you see
Which are my specific selections.

The first to be banned are the critters
And although there are some that I love
They're excluded here
And I make my point clear
Cause it is sex in the title above.

So it's clear that I have no interest
In things that stay in their pens
Though I must admit
This group is a fit
For some of my lower class friends.

The next subject to take our attention
Though it's deemed not an option by some
The decision to render
Is exactly which gender
You would choose to be opposite from.

For me, I don't have a question
It's the ladies that I just adore
So I here will relate
I believe that I'm straight
And I'm much disinclined to explore.

But the ladies, the ladies, the ladies
I don't think I'm being extreme
Each shape and size
In its own way a prize
An answer to some man's dream.

But the subject is sex, I regress
I'll focus and keep it in mind
The myriad ways
The sex game plays
And revel in each special kind.

First we'll have understanding
Of the rules that do not exist
There is sex of a sort
That's a non-contact sport
(Though it's rather far down on my list).

This is letters and songs and poems
From afar they reach in and touch
In a place we keep
Whatever's down deep
Maybe that's why we feel it so much.

But it does touch, and further, it moves us
And albeit it's done from distance
The feelings inside
Can't be denied
It melts a cold hearts resistance.

But fighting the cold's better done
With a touch, an embrace or a kiss
Best for sex to begin
With skin touching skin
To remind us of touching we miss.

And don't use a kiss as a key
To enter a place lesser known
For the kiss in itself
Is a fountain of wealth
To buy passion where passion is grown.

And not every kiss leads to passion
There's a kiss to say each different thing
Goodbye or hello
Or, please, just go slow
Wordless messages soft lips can bring.

Here while we've discounted passion
Think of hands upon hands or a shoulder
To just say that you're near
Or there's no need to fear
Are conveyed without words, which are colder.

But let us bring back the passion
That blinds us… and brings us to see
Two beings combine
In a feeling sublime
And makes us all we can be.

To touch the nipple electric
Lightly touch the smoothness with care
To freely express
The deep tenderness
And show all the feeling that's there.

And then, the acts of abandon
Tsunami emotions they flow
And passions whirl
With this heaving girl
I am spent with a glory I know.

But sex, it's still not over
Beside you a life form divine
And you don't turn away
And you won't turn away
And in your exhaustion you find,

A throat with a pulse you can feel
With your lips and the tip of your tongue
Taste the sweet salt of sweat
By the passion beget
And be glad that the night is still young.

For she will envelop, enfold you
Take control with a soft velvet glove
And she'll whisper to you
What she all the time knew
That this isn't sex... this is love.

GRAY LOVE

There's a line somewhere that says
Youth on the young is wasted
And the same is true of love
Like a fine wine drunk untasted

When passions rage unfettered
The passion's what you feel
And the gentleness of love
Is more implied than real

That's not to say it won't be there
When those passions cool
But to say you have it all in youth
Is the wisdom of a fool

For love in later life
Although the passion's there
Is savored in its action
Much more to feel and share

With age there comes the knowledge
That as you quaff the wine
That bottle soon will empty
As we all run out of time

So each word each act each touch
That might in youth be missed
Is treasured when you're older
Causing pleasure to persist

So loving in the later years
Instead of less is more
With a fuller appreciation
Of what makes love endure

THE LOOK

It is in your eyes, I see it
Could it be my ego, no.
For no matter how inflated
It couldn't dream you so.

It is in your eyes, I see it
You hold me gently there
And warm my heart inside me
With the hungry brown eyed stare.

No hunger born of lack I see
But fulfillment yet to sate
But yearns and pines and thanks
For our feelings that relate.

Relate they do, concordant
And in my eyes she'll see
The lust and love and serenity
She creates inside of me.

JOYS END

When the western sky assembles
To bid adieu the setting sun
The colors for me will be filtered
Through the sunset, set for one.

Hers were times I shared this glory
The vastness made us close
Now the loveliness of the sunset
Is the time I miss her most.

The sun sinks low into the sky
Paints the clouds a salmon glow
And offers colors yet unnamed
But there's no one else to know.

So I solo with the sunset
And yes I'm glad I'm there
But its beauty would be multiplied
Were she here with me to share.

COMPULSION

Has the door been locked
Has it really been done?
I'll check again I'm the cautious one
I could have checked it
A little time ago
But I must check again
It's for sure I've got to know.

My friends say I am skinny
I think I'm much too fat
So I'll skip my meat and pasta
Diet cola's where it at.
And if I'm very careful
I'll lose the fat I see
And have before me in the mirror
The shape I want to be.

I forget, did I wash my hands
After coming through the door?
I really can't remember
And I really must be sure.
I scrubbed them well enough
The last time, I would guess
To rid them of the "others" stuff
That infests this filthy mess.

One more piece of cake
Before I end the night
I won't have any breakfast
And that will make it right
According to the diet book
If I should cheat a bit
I shouldn't be discouraged
I can make up for it.

My desk is in a shambles
My pencil is askew
The fringe around my rug
Is major messed up too
How can I be expected
To perform my best unless
They think my mind is just as fouled
As is this awful mess

There are compulsions and compulsions
That never give us rest
That we must lose or learn to live with
To have a life that's best
But I have my compulsion
It's a compulsion that I choose
My compulsion is to love her
A compulsion I won't lose.

ENCORE

I drift back from my slumber and become aware.
Aware of my contentment
In the now flickering candlelight.
Aware of the sweet warmth that is still beside me.
Tenderness overwhelms me
And I turn toward you.

Now, in the soft glow of candle light
The passion long subsided.
I can see your back and shoulder
And your tousled hair.
Your skin so soft,
Is now dry and cool to touch,
And you, in your naked innocence,
Are sleeping.
I kiss your shoulder, oh so softly,
You groan and nestle closer.

The scent of you, your body, your hair
Pervades my senses.
As I lay so close,
Can you feel my heart pounding?
My hand leaves your shoulder
And gently traces the feminine line
Beneath the covers
Your hip, your waist, your ribs
And forward to your breast.

I touch you gently, just for me
For you are still asleep.
I press you to me and kiss your back again,
Perhaps less softly…
And you stir—you press with yours
The hand that cups your breast.
You twist, and turn,
And are in my arms again.

REPLACED PRONOUN

I told her,
It wasn't what she said
But rather her response to me
That had me forge ahead

For me, I felt my obligation
To tell her who could care
To whom she could rely upon
Who always would be there.

And yet she told another
That he was just like them
And they were not reliable
She would not try again.

For her I was persistent
I tried, and it was hard you see
To tell her I love you
She had to be for me

I told her this was our time
This time was made for us
She and I should be together
And remain forever thus.

And over time she changed
It's no longer her and me
Our she and I are missing
Replaced by a better we.

SAY IT

When words fail… say them
Don't be mute by choice
The poor and bumbling phrasing
May be your feeling's only voice.

If emotion numbs the intellect
You must force the thought to word
No matter how your heart cries out
You must speak to have it heard.

Who can construe a silence
To mean the things you feel
You must speak the words inside you
In order to make them real.

You would choose more polished phrases
Yours are overused and trite
But they're the only words you have
Saying them makes them right.

Don't criticize the verbiage
The words you have will do
How many ways can you couch the thought
My darling… I love you.

CHAPTER 5

Look and See

DARK GARDEN

A crescent moon in star-lit skies,
A garden path lit by fireflies,
A profusion of roses, an artist's delight,
Obscured from view by the cloak of night.

Slim scimitar moon carves this night,
And twinkling stars give too little light
So daytime flowers are lost to you now,
Yet the garden's still beautiful, but why, and how?

It's the night's sweet breath in this garden spot,
Perfumed by weeds on a vacant lot,
Where by the confusion of vines you'll know
That's where the honeysuckles grow.

TRANSITION

The dawn is here
And yet not quite,
Slowly drags The hem of night.
Confusion reigns
Who holds sway
Retreating night
Or advancing day?

FLOWERS

Their subtle fragrance fills the air
Their vivid colors everywhere
Not free; this beauty asks its due
The pollen count—my God, kerchoo!

THE GRACEFUL TRAVELER

A gull is soaring overhead;
The picture of effortless grace.
He dips and banks and soars again,
As he slips from the wind's embrace.

Silently, he plies his trade,
A sailor on a colorless sea;
'Till this sloop of the sky has sailed away,
Away from earth-bound me.

PRE-WINTER RAIN

Blue-gray sky on a dreary day,
Muddy roads to bar our way,
Soggy shoes and sodden head,
As rain beats down from clouds of lead.

Slanting rain keeps coming down
On the shed's tin roof, makes a drumming sound,
Not the cadence of march is beat,
But more the tempo of dreams sans sleep.

The fire's lit, the first since spring,
The whistling teapot starts to sing;
A cozy warmth pervades this room
Oblivious to the outside's gloom.

AN EQUATION

My favorite time is spring
It's fulfillment of a promise
With the rush of growing green
'Till July beats down upon us.

Summer is my second best,
I enjoy its sultry night,
With mirrored moon in the lily pond
Passed by clouds in flight.

I've little regard for autumn
As days terse and crisper grow,
A facade of wildly colored leaves,
A clown with tears that show.

Winter, you ignorant tyrant
Your only saving grace,
That close on the heels of your rampage
Comes my spring to take your place.

COME QUICKLY PRINCE

I am expecting spring
It never comes too soon,
For if my will were forced on the world
For twelve full months we'd have June.

But I'm more than accepting of summer,
Another luxurious season.
With its lazy days and sultry nights
It's my second choice with reason.

The months of fall have their color,
This only a fool could deny,
But their beauty is like a viewing
For those leaves about to die.

Then comes the long, cold winter,
Could any fate be worse
Than to freeze our Mother Nature
Into Sleeping Beauty's curse?

But the sun is our Prince Charming,
And with his boldly lengthening days,
He'll soon scale that terrible tower
Where spring's Sleeping Beauty lays.

Yes, soon upon her frozen lips
His awakening kiss will be pressed
Then he, and all the rest of us,
Will with all her beauty be blessed.

ONE SMALL CANDLE

I chanced to pass a rubbish dump,
A sorry sight to see
This picture of dirt and rubble
Brought no happiness to me.

When a bit of brightness caught my eye
And bid me closer view..
But, It was only a dandelion
Sprinkled with morning dew.

But no roses twined around that junk,
No pampered posies bloomed,
Just broken bottles, cans, and rust,
And one flower to break the gloom,

So I looked again at that lowly weed
That is cursed in every lawn,
And gave thanks for the flower that fought for life,
And brought beauty, where beauty had gone.

DISGUISE

Your roses red as rubies,
Your diamond dew drops gleam,
Your soft green velvet mosses,
Are you quite what you seem?

Your raiment ragged as the leaves,
Belie the clues we've seen,
I believe our Mother Nature
Is an incognito Queen.

DAYS END

It had mellowed in its age
Its labor nearly done
Now permitted views of glory
As it had when day begun.

Sliding down the western sky
Its descent is gaining speed
This marvelous star that warms us
Gives us beauty we must heed

Admit that there are colors
That no palette can conceive
Be painfully aware that,
When it's gone there's no reprieve

In it's waning moments
As it lets the daylight die
We must attend the moment's magic
And wonder at the sky.

CHAPTER 6

Just to Entertain

GERMS

My nose is running
My eyes feel dry
It's hard to swallow
And I know why

My throat is raspy
My headache pounds
I'm attacked by the bug
That is going around

It's not the usual adult stuff
That has me on the skids
It's that wildly virulent brand
That comes from little kids

They come around and sniffle
Those pint-sized petri dishes
And lay the germs upon me
Against my pleas and wishes

Little faces flushed with fever
I feel sorry but it's scary
This draggy little darling
Is in fact a Typhoid Mary

In a day or two this little runt
Will be chipper, and past this germ
But I his loving teacher
Will feel lousy for the term

I am well aware there's more to come
For this is just the first
They'll bring me more and better germs
And I will feel much worse.

DEMIGOD

His demeanor is not cold
It's that he is so aloof
It's my inferiority
He needs no other proof

There are times he talks
But only when I err
He chides the signs of laxness
When he sees that fault occur

He knows how small are his demands
He expects that they be met
With proper timing and decorum
He should deserve and get

I try, I really try
To avoid that patient stare
To have his things together
When he's ready for them there

I do my best to serve him
With small reward or none
And yet I'm criticized
For what I haven't done

The only time I know
This regal stuffed chair sitter
Is something less than royal…
When I dump the kitty litter.

CHARACTER FLAWS

Some of us are flawed
In ways that don't offend.
But jeopardize our lives
If the flaws we don't amend.

To smile a friendly smile
On the street or on a bus
To God forbid a stranger
Is perilous to us.

For who knows what dark secret
What evil and deceit
That now is loosed upon us
By that smile so indiscreet.

There are dangers lurking everywhere
Strangers with every vice.
So mend your ways, be careful
And just don't be so nice.

ANTS

In the vastness of the Universe
As if by master Plan,
A star explodes with titanic force
To belittle insignificant man.

But this egotistical creature
Still toys with Nature's might,
His pipe dreams outdistance his knowledge
Like a snail racing beams of light.

Yet forever he meddles and blunders,
Imagination, ambition waxing hot,
In search of some sort of power
To transport him someplace he's not.

Yet someday, with space ships and rockets
He'll travel to Venus and Mars,
But that won't still the ants in his pants,
He'll then have to reach for the stars.

So perhaps in the year of one million
In this whole Universe you'll see,
Each galaxy bathed in the rosy glow
Of earthman's idiocy.

LOVE THY NEIGHBOR

According to the good books tenets
Our enemies we should forgive
Return their malice with love
We're supposed to live and let live.

But for me, this plan doesn't work
There are folks I just plain despise
And I don't wish them well and I won't wish them well
And those feelings I'm loath to disguise.

I really and truly don't like them.
I avoid any chance of our meeting.
Just stay away... forever I pray
Their misfortune for me is a greeting.

The effect of this bile I carry?
Those people don't give a damn.
They go through their lives as smoothly as silk
And surely don't care who I am.

But for those that I really do care for
It is strange but it's certainly true.
I find myriad ways to distress them
With the thoughtless things that I do.

So the good book has the solution.
Give your love, it says, to the heathen.
I should do it soon, I should do it now,
And then I'll get righteous... and even.

OFFENCE

At the beach I saw a girl
And I said she was beautiful
I was scolded, because she was more
She had a mind.

My friend bought a car
And I said I liked the color
He scolded me, it was more
It had 300 horsepower.

My aunt brought the turkey to the table
I said it looked delicious
And she scolded me, it was more
She said it was nutritious.

My grandma had a garden
And I said the roses were beautiful
She scolded me
Because her tomatoes were prizewinners.

If something that I like appears
Should I not say I like that
For fear of scolding
For my selection of what to admire?

I think not.

YOU SAY HE WANTS TO KNOW?

If you and your spouse will just agree
I will tell him of your time with me
I will tell him of the days and nights
Forbidden times of rare delights
Of lying in the warming sun
Of plans we made and left undone
All these things I'll blithely tell
Sure I will…
I will like hell!

EDUCATION

There was terror in the night for me
Each shadow, ogre-filled!
'Till a gentle grown-up lit the light,
And then my fears were stilled.

Not just the room was lighted,
But the darkness of my mind
That placed the monsters in the night
For a frightened child to find.

Now, softly, darkness stalks me,
It finds me unafraid
Of the friendly shadows in the room
Where my bed is made.

CHAPTER 7

Have a Thought

WARM BEER

May old friends never meet
Except at time or place,
Where now again with things in common,
Their old paths they retrace,

Better never meet again,
This friend from time gone by,
Who sparks no fire of camaraderie
No matter how we try.

Parted, friends won't stay the same,
We change with every day,
It's best to just not meet again,
And let fond memories stay.

POV

When the petals have fallen,
And you are asked,
Is that rose beautiful?
If you should say it is...
Is it beautiful,
As a duty to its past,
Or for the promise of its future?

If you believe that the beauty
Of the rose that is no more
Is in the promise of the future
You have the eyes of youth
And are blessed with hope.
And if you say as a duty to the past
You do not have the eyes of youth
But hoard for your self memories...
And beauty will always be with you.

And if you say the rose
That is no more
Is gone, and has no beauty.
You are trapped in the present
Cursed with reality.
Sans hope, sans memories.

FOR SALE, TWO PICTURES

Solid, hard, city of concrete.
Unfeeling, unfelt, beneath uncaring feet.

Moist, molding, humus cradles seed.
Answered, answering, whatever life may need.

Honking horns screeching brakes,
The disciplined din a railroad makes.
Glaring neon spewing light,
Making a mockery of night.

A sheltered stream gurgles along,
Providing rhythm for the night birds song,
Frogs in chorus, solo loon,
Serenade an attentive moon.

A drunk is in the doorway,
Bloody lip and blackened eye...
Beset by hoodlums of the night,
And left, perhaps to die.

The moon smiles on the meadow
As the doe suckles spotted fawn
And rabbits frisk around the glade
Until the night is gone.

Now you've seen my pictures sir,
And if the price you'll give,
I'll deliver you sir,

To where the pictures live.

THE MARKER

"... *Round the decay*
Of that colossal wreck, boundless and bare
The lone and level sands stretch far away."
Percy Bysshe Shelley

I see you, Ozymandias,
Colossus in the sand,
I gaze with curious wonder
At the face that ruled this land.

Ozymandias, I am afraid,
Not of cities sacked and burned,
But a much more terrible terror
Of a lesson still unlearned.

I am fearful, Ozymandias,
That in this barren land,
Is not the wreck of Ozymandias,
But a monument to man.

AND A TIME TO DIE

Have you ever thought of the pity
We've just one life to live,
When some great person passes on,
Who had much more to give?

If they only had another day
To complete the task they try,
But their light is lost to all of us,
For, like us all, they die.

The scientist will seek no more
Though the problem's end is near.
His puzzlement solved by someone else
But it's answers not quite so clear.

And who could complete the music
That the master left undone
As he wrote with such color and feeling
In the light of life's fading sun.

Some things cannot be finished,
Some others, poorly, at best.
For the ones who know and those who feel
Are laid too soon to rest.

But is there a brave one among us
To part with life's quick running sand?
Who would give a grain, who would give an hour,
Of his life to another man?

I beg, think before you answer,
Take time to ponder, my friend.
This hour, if offered is not from now
But from dear life's very end.

Providence grants us a favor,
That decision's not ours to make,
A higher power than our poor minds
Says who, or who not, to take.

GENIUS

Through the space
Of the human race
An occasional comet gleams.
Why this glory
Is an untold story,
Is this void more dense than it seems?

What sparked that flame,
From whence it came?
Are answers we laymen desire.
Did it glow that way
From its very first day,
Or did something ignite that fire?

If we could learn
What makes them burn,
If it's something not inborn, but done,
We could light this space
Of the whole human race,
Make it glow like one glorious sun.

THE POWER

Perhaps the greatest gift
That God has given man
Is the ability to appreciate
The things his senses span.

Much more beautiful is the sunset
If you'll only keep in mind
How drab and dull that sky would be
Were you simply colorblind.

Be sensitive to things around you,
The subtleties don't overlook,
The fragrance of pines in the forest,
Or the murmurings of a brook.

They're there. You can hear, and smell, and see.
But what makes these boons so great
Is not just sensing all these things
But the power to appreciate.

WHAT IS NOT DAVID

The thought of potlatch was disturbing...

To give up all you had.
For what? I could not see.
To give up all my worldly goods

It made no sense to me.

The Buddhists with their beggar bowls...

To live that way
With less than hand to mouth
With saffron robe and empty bowl
How did that come about?

The harangue I hear is to simplify...

They say that less is more
That extras, they confuse
Get down to your essence
And what you need to use.

Perhaps philosophy leaves me cold...

And maybe that's the reason
It took another way
For me to understand
Just what they had to say.

For then came my insight with David...
And that what is not David has import...

He stands there perfect in form
Of a million stone chips he is free
What is not David is gone
The perfection remains what we see.
Only now you can see
How it cluttered the space
Hid the soul of the stone
And that fabulous face.

It concealed the body divine
All of that beauty and grace
A malevolent mass of rock
That the artist's skill would erase.

Still, with potlatch I am disturbed...

I lack the courage (or the wisdom)
To shuck off frills I find
Yet retain the phrase of "less is more"
In the echoes of my mind.

And it echoes and echoes and echoes...

A child with a thousand toys
He sulks through a boring day
Yet a girl with her single dolly
Rapt attention for what it might say.

And it echoes and echoes and echoes...

In her mansion with servants and pool
A headache keeps her inside
When another tends the small garden
The garden, her cottage's pride.

And it echoes and echoes and echoes...

The rock star has his groupies
Variety the spice of his life
Yet I have the ultimate Eden
In "quality time" with my wife.

And it echoes and echoes and echoes....

FOR THE SAKE OF NEATNESS

Freshly cut and bound
The cords of wood are stacked
No room for knot or gnarl,
So closely are they packed.

Discard the twisted bough
Omit that knotty piece,
So the uniformity of the pile
Is disturbed not in the least.

Two people pick the cast-off pile,
The boughs, the sculptor's lot,
And the foolish smithy's helper
Takes all the rest that's knot.

SOME FABLES

Poor apple at approaching winter
Sparer, and yet sparer, with gnarled arthritic limbs,
Leaf by leaf appearing more senile
Clacking in the wind.

Sprightly spruce in dark green coat
That reaches to the ground,
Fully muffled, head to toe,
And a hat with a pointed crown.

One won't see the spring.

FOR MERCY SAKE

Is euthanasia such a terrible thing
To a tortured body, rest and comfort bring
From an earthbound Hell, that soul release
Let that troubled spirit go in search of peace?

There are glorious castles beyond our ken
With splendor and beauty undreamed of by men,
Where loved ones departed forever wait
For our lives to be plucked from us by Fate.

But the cry is "No!" that life don't take.
It's yourself to a God you're trying to make,
This may, in part, perhaps be true,
It's what a merciful God would do.

So, on their deathbed, loved ones remain
Knowing nothing else but pain,
Kept alive by science as days go by,
Denied the luxury to die.

Now who plays God, is all I ask,
This heartless Science, I'll take to task,
They'll stretch life beyond hope's end
While I to our God a soul would send.

FLY EAST

If you awake and darkness
Makes useless seeing eyes,
Unfold your wings and journey
To the glowing eastern skies.

Leave the night; go seek the light
As did three wiser men;
For no one knows that hour
We'll be made to sleep again.

EXPERIMENT IN TIME

The reality of being
What does it mean to you
To be, or not to be
Does it shape the things you do?

Down to the very basis
Of the things that you believe
The now and the hereafter
The existence you perceive.

For only in this thinking
Can you truly then decide
How to shape your living
The behavior you'll abide.

Without this thoughtful process
Your not far removed from ape
For man's the only animal
Who's aware there's no escape.

Man understands mortality
Or can, it's better said
When he brings himself to think
After living we are dead.

And when he does this thinking
First comes the childlike fear
Of all that is unknowable
When we're no longer here.

But later in this process
Comes the calm and inner peace
Knowing things in his control
Before that last release.

Then he really lives
With knowledge and desire
Dispensing then with pettiness
Before the quenching of life's fire.

Each day as it passes
Is enjoyed more than before
For then it's truly savored
In memory twice explored.

If there is a good to do
It's harder to postpone
You know you've got to get it done
For "too late" is not known.

Thus time itself is changed
Both gained and lost import
With the paradox of feeling
For life that's deemed too short.

So the key is in expenditure
That time is wisely spent
Judicious choices rendered
In this last experiment.

For if you think, then you can choose
With no need to repent
The way you guide your actions
In this last experiment.

CHAPTER 8

Introspection

MY POEMS

Are ones that do not shout or sulk
Or pretend to be more than me
(My ego and my pride Forbid that trespass)
I would have them enjoyed
For what they may contain…
My thought, my feeling
Or my anguish
And not have them disdained
For their lack of literary merit.
For they are not meant to be meritorious
They are me, and what I see.

MY ARMIES

Shimmering silks resplendent
Over link and armor steel
With lance and rapier ready,
I await the trumpets' peal.

At last, that note is sounded.
Do I charge to sure defeat,
With my glorious rhyming Armies
On their mandarin metrical feet?

A ROAD NOT TAKEN

I travel a lonely highway
With all the human race;
No notion where I'm going,
Nor who has set the pace.

I keep in step as best I can
Though cadence I can't hear
By watching feet of fellows
In the rank I'm marching near.

From a distance, I see road signs,
Hopes buoy spirits high;
I'll soon know where I'm going,
And, maybe, even why.

But I'm doomed to disappointment
When the signs come into view,
They all have the same trite message:
"It all depends on you."

Still I tramp this highway, thinking,
"It can't be them… it's me"
'Til a voice from down inside me says
"Like lemmings to the sea."

If courage I'm not granted
To break my stride and turn
To a by-way more appealing,
Why must these questions burn?

If courage is not granted,
Why not, in recompense,
At least my rightful measure
Of the bliss of ignorance.

JUST FOR THE RECORD

I keep a daily diary,
Or should say, it's kept for me,
My every action logged,
No matter what it be.

Oh, yes, I did a favor
While I was on my way,
Was that my saving grace
For the wrongs I did today?

This I'll know tomorrow,
Diary pages on display,
As I see the smiles or frowns
On the faces I meet today.

ENTER EDUCATION

I sing a song of a wastrel son
A melody ended before its been sung,
Of a child bride to an ancient king,
A sudden autumn in a year sans spring.

I went aloft on waxen wings
When other lads were creeping,
I rendezvoused with unknown things
When all about were sleeping.

I traveled in my flights
From pit to pole somehow
Until I found it;
The book; the sun is now.

With it open I dare not fly
Even though the sky is brightened
And closed… I choose to sulk,
Mute, but still enlightened.

WOMEN'S LOOKS
(Extrinsic Validation Problem)

Not how they look but how they looked,
It's changed a lot some how.
From times gone by when I was young
To how they're looking now.

First it was great big ladies,
Who ogled and laughed with me.
Who chucked my chin and patted my cheek,
And I knew what it felt like to be.

I saw eyes 'round corners, over books,
Through fingers and their hair.
Shy smiles on rougeless lips,
And I could tell that I was there.

Then furtive eyes through lashes,
With just a hint of spice.
Suggesting a half known question,
I was there, and it was nice.

Then the eyes that looked at me…
And then they looked away.
That almost spoke a whispered word
I was there, and knew just what they'd say.

Later still another look…
Part quizzical, part a challenge stare.
Full, direct, that rhetorical question posed.
I know for I was there.

Now the looks, most all have stopped.
They're not nasty, it seems they just don't care.
It appears like age and glasses
Makes me feel that I'm not there.

THE WITNESS

For my writing endeavors
I choose poetry
I use rhyme and meter
And that seems right for me.

Oh, I write some in freeform
But the meter mostly stays
And I try to make it understood
Just what my poem says.

I don't hide a secret thought
Or try to be obscure
I just plain lay it out
So you'll understand I'm sure

I don't think that you're stupid
That you need this clarity
But why should you work to understand
What happens inside of me?

If I can make it clearer
With another verse that's good
I gladly take this extra step
And I really think I should

‘Cause if I have an idea
That’s worth the time to write
I want to have it understood
Even if a little trite.

So if you read a poem of mine
You’ll know the story I’m telling
And if you don’t you can be sure
It’s just my lousy spelling.

And if in recitation
It’s unclear what you heard
I guarantee the problem is
I’ve mispronounced a word.

Communication is the word.
There are no puzzles here
I want all to understand
And have my meanings clear.

So if my meter bores you
And rhyming rubs you raw
Perhaps I’m not poet, but a witness
To the wonders that I saw.

SEARCHING

So filled with discontent am I
That it borders on despair,
And it doesn't leave
But continues to grieve
When I go anywhere.

My good wife's patience is sorely tried
Along with others about,
Though I try to hide
What's down inside
The bitterness lashes out.

Why all this restless boiling?
Why, oh why, all the bile?
Why the bitter seeds
Of thoughtless deeds?
Or to hurt for the lack of a smile?

I should be thankful for what I have,
For friends, and a wife who is good,
And forget the taste
Of that feeling of waste,
Oh lord, how I wish that I could.

Perhaps my affliction is caused
By an ego so swollen in size
It won't let me rest'
'Till I've passed some test,
Or won some coveted prize.

But I can think of no trophy
And can really imagine no test,
What I do want to do
My whole life through,
Is whatever I truly do best.

BEGGAR FOR THE MOON

I'm living just one life,
Would God would grant me more,
To question, hope, feel and love,
Past my ten and just three score.

Not merely life, I'm asking,
No sterile mental state,
But a rollicking, bloody bout with life
...That I can win... I beg from Fate.

IN MEMORY

A year has passed since our battlers gone
To a place we might never know,
A place that's reserved for the strong at heart,
Where the true believers go.

Yet I think of the child who's no longer here,
Can I help but be bitter and mourn,
Easily forgotten, he's gone to a place
Where his pain need no longer be borne.

God forgive these bitter tears,
They're a mother's tears of love,
Who feels her son was taken too soon
To meet with God above.

(Written for Jimmy and his Mom Edna.)

WHAT'S LEFT

The old old man breathes heavily
(He had leaned over from his chair
To pick up the newspaper from the floor)
He's almost out of breath.

The old man, he looks eighty-five
But he's just over fifty
And shiny-top bald-headed
(He always was as I remember)

The strong jaw and cleft chin
Now frail, cheeks and eyes sunk in.
The powerful form now parodied
By the telling barrel chest.

Over the top of his glasses
He grins… maybe he leers.
"How come you are going out now
When respectable people are coming home."

"I ain't respectable pop…
It's in my genes"
And I am gone.
He would have liked to talk.

But we talked often…
"Got five bucks till payday pop?"
"Only three."

And I never paid him back.

There were times before the ending
When he told of inventions
Never patented
That are used across the land.

Of tricks of engineering
That made things break
Out where they could be fixed
Not down in their guts.

Of prize fighters who really could be good
If only they would train harder,
Or eat less, or leave the girls alone,
Or had stronger bones in their hands.

He was not all talk, when young
He would lie on the floor
Face up, hands above his head.
And he would make an arch.

Only backs of hands and heels touching floor
To prove it not a fluke he would face down
And arch, only hands and toes touching the floor.
Nothing else… that's power.

And in the ending, when the drugs
Made his thinking less that true
He believed that the young nurse
(Loretta I believe)
Was, by prescription, he thought,
Supposed to lie with him for comfort.
Of this delirium she was aware
And she smiled and was kind to him.

But he was aware of his condition
And knew he could not lie with her
So he asked his son to take his medication.
And he put our hands together across his covers.

She was lovely, she smiled at him and me
And suggested "at another time."
Thus assured that that sweet Potent would not waste
He went to sleep.

But mostly I remember the gasping for breath
The mouth wide to optimize the flow of air.
That would not optimize.
Ever.

And he would tease or crack a joke
Or be interested in me, or he, or she
And have a word of optimism
For whomever.

And I asked him as he suffered
How can you be pleasant
In the ponderous discomfort
Of your struggle for every breath?

And he told me, what he believed the truth.
That no one has it bad enough
That they have the right
To be a grouch.

And that belief is
What's left for me.

CHAPTER 9

Stories

FLIGHT TO HIROSHIMA

The night was not for sleeping
As I watched the moon shine down,
Reflecting an eerie brilliance
From the bombers on the ground.

This tropic night is peaceful,
Yet Fate must turn its page,
For tonight is simply August Fifth,
But tomorrow's, 'the Atom Age'.

A year ago we started
With the flying Army's best
To try and train, to try and build,
The men to stand this test.

Of the many that ran the gauntlet
Just three crews are left,
For now their flying's precision,
Each maneuver deft.

Now tonight becomes tomorrow
The waiting is all done.
We're to fly our birds of shining steel
To the Land of the Rising Sun.

There's no sound of roaring engines
When flying up so high
For we must carry this seed of death
Six miles up in the sky.

Now the day is dawning
It's the sun of Nippon's pride.
Before this sun has set again,
How many will have died?

Twenty-five miles to target
With sweat my brow's abead
What will my place in humanity be
After doing this terrible deed?

Will I be looked upon with revulsion,
And called the Butcher supreme
Oh, Lord, that I would awaken
Like a child from a horrible dream.

But I know that this is no nightmare,
For the bomb has just been dropped
And although my watch keeps ticking,
I feel that time has stopped.

My God The bomb has exploded.
All Hades on Earth is massed,
On one tiny spot on the face of the globe,
The point of that fabulous blast.

Now, the silence is deafening,
As that mushroom rises to air
And at times like this there's no other thought
Than the thought of silent prayer.

Oh, please, make this the last one
To end forevermore
That terrible disease that follows man,
That plague that's known as war.

Oh please make this the last one
And let God look down and see
That we can live together as brothers
The way he meant us to be.

THE CURSE OF THE FLYING DUTCHMAN

It was three hundred years ago
A galleon sailed the Main,
When ere it met another ship,
The seas blood red were stained.

They never took a captive
In all their sailing years,
And to be the Dutchman's prize
Was the worst of the seaman's fears.

They'll never get to Heaven,
The old, old sailors tell,
They're doomed to sail their gory bark
Till their souls are damned to Hell.

So, sailor, show some pity,
No matter who may ask,
For if your work is not for God,
The Devil sets your task.

Heed my word, you sailor man,
I am one to know.
I killed a man in yonder port,
And now to sea must go...

Now the day is dying,
The night will bring no cheer,
I fear the mists are coming,
And the Dutchman will be near.

He's here to claim a crewman,
I'm no better than his worse;
I killed a man in cold, cold blood,
Now I own that seaman's curse.

Oh, the Dutchman's crew is chosen,
So the old, old sailors tell,
From the dregs of man, to sail the sea
Till their souls are damned to hell.

So, sailor, show some pity,
No matter who may ask,
For if your work is not for God,
The Devil sets your task.

TRADING POST

Spotted pony on a snowy hill,
Indian brave in the winter's chill,
Cold and gaunt in the freezing snow,
They gaze at the White-eyes' Fort below.

There most of his people leave wigwams cold,
Turn their backs on the ways of the Red Man of old,
Beg from the White-eyes, like papoose from a squaw,
Forgetful of pride and of tribal law.

Tribal law is written, and true,
Your duty's to fight one who steals from you,
But it's hard to think of valorous deeds,
When warmth and food are such urgent needs.

Poor pony's head dips lower yet,
Will hunger and cold make this brave forget?
He's a prince among men, a leader, a chief,
Will he fetter his pride for the white man's relief?

He looks at the stars, his decision made,
Knowing at least he has something to trade,
For that comfort that comes from an honorable bed
Barter, war whoop and charge...for a half ounce of lead.

The night is rent with a hideous yell,
The savage attacks like a demon from Hell
The Fort is alert now, the guards are keen,
The raiders are heard, but not yet seen.

At last one sentinel draws a bead
On a figure approaching at breakneck speed,
The Savages' Leader his hand held high
Brandishing war spear against the sky.

A perfect target on a night like this,
A shot rings out that can't possibly miss.
The marksman's sure his shot ended a raid,
When in reality there's just been a trade.

THE TRIP

No McKay County, I welcome YOU
Your macadam highway is an appreciated change
From the whurr flap whurr flap whurr flap
Of that damn old concrete road.

I can finally hear the radio play…
For how long, who knows
FM's clear but it drops you like a stone
When you get too far.

In this part of the country
Stations are spaced
Hell, everything is spaced
Towns don't blend together here
Like they do in Jersey

There are lights ahead
They have the iridescence of opals
In their colored halos.
I don't remember whether,
When I was much younger,
If those halos existed
Or is this an aberration of age.
Not every thing is worse with age.

Plenty of gas
Glad I don't have a gas hog anymore
It's much cheaper to travel now
But it sure keeps me aware
Of my lack of bladder size

One truck in the last twenty minutes
No cars—no worthwhile radio
Man, this ride is smooth…

Eighty-five miles an hour smooth
Get off it or some local fuzz
Will feast on you tonight

Sixty-five is respectable and fast enough
Better than a mile a minute
Is a no stress ride.

"If I had a nickel I tell you what I'd do
I'd spend it all on candy
And give it all to you
For that's how much I love you baby
That's how much I love you"

I know there's more to that than that
"If I had a"… quarter? dollar?

Damn... ti dum ti dum

"I had a dream dear
You had one too
Mine was the best dream
Because
It was
Of you"

Big deal, you're better than me
I knew that
But I don't like to be told.
I would tell you
But I don't like to be told.

Attend! Something up ahead
A white flash on the dark road
Avoid!
...Poor squashed skunkie
Phew but doesn't that
Clear your sinuses
I'm glad I missed him
The car would reek for a week.

Another truck...
They are my low beams stupid!
There, that's better.

People say there's no trust anymore
I just passed that truck
A relative speed over a hundred miles per hour
That's trust...

Jeez, when you think about it
Even in the neighborhood
The relative speed is fifty
Everybody trusts They just don't know it

"If I had a million
I tell you what I'd do
I'd buy myself an airplane
And fly right home to you"...

Da ta da...

"Fly the ocean in a golden plane
See the... what's it?
When it's wet with rain
Just remember...
De da home—till you're home again
You belong to me...

- - -

Impact... Massive force...
And I can't comprehend
I can't comprehend, and I can't move,
Can't see, can't hear, can't feel.

I CAN smell.
Smell that sweet oiliness
Of steam and anti-freeze.

I CAN move.
My right arm,
And my tongue.
Nothing else.
My mouth has a strangeness
That my tongue inspects, unbidden.

My left side teeth
And upper jaw are gone.
My right arm
Can reach my forehead
Touch my left brow
To where it ends
And there is nothing
But jagged bone
Past my mid left brow.

Where is the pain?
Where is the terror?
I was cheated
No life flashed
Before my eyes.
I just wait.

Too weak to raise my arm again
To test my brow for better news.
My hand is in my lap
My legs bound together
In a steel cocoon.

My lap is full of warmth
And wetness.
Pee or blood?
No matter,
Where is the pain?
And I am weary.

I am weary and
I hope soon to sleep.
Before the pain finds me…

Go to sleep…

"If I had a nickel
I tell you"…

I tell you
My epitaph…

Jackass…
Asleep at the wheel.

THROUGH PURGATORY

Caught between that searing sun
And oven earth, am I.
Trapped in this fearsome furnace
Of scorched sand and burning sky.

The heat flows over me in waves
Like the surf in a sea of flame,
And to quaff this fire with my poor parched mouth
Is to bathe my throat in pain.

How much further can it be
To that horrid place I dread?
Close at hand to where I plod,
Or yon mirage of molten lead?

No vultures yet defile the sky—
I'm stronger than I think
Yet it seems like days or weeks have passed
Since I measured my last drink.

My lips are cracked, my mouth is dry,
My eyes seem filled with sand,
On my Mother's grave, oh why in hell
Did I come to this cursed land?

Nuggets of gold, of solid gold,
I said for sure I'd find,
I had a map to lead me
To the old lost Dutchman's Mine.

I had a map to lead me,
It led through an arid maze
Of canyons gullies, hills and plains
For five confusing days.

Then after five I wandered
And with my incredible luck
I found the spot on devil's mount
The bonanza the Dutchman struck.

I laughed and swore like a madman
Till a mental picture loomed,
Of a horrible grinning skeleton
In the Dutchman's mine entombed.

The specter with the grizzly grin...
My mind knew who he'd be.... .
If I tarried with this gold
That skeleton was me.

Off food, canteens, and blankets,
Dispense with these mundane things
I packed my poor old burro
Heavy with the wealth of kings.

Wealth alone won't make you wise,
The reverse for me was true,
I hadn't trekked too very far
Till the fool I'd been I knew.

My burro brayed for water,
I had not planned for him,
My filled canteen was just for me,
And the margin there was slim.

Six buckets of gold on a burro
A burro whose mouth had dried,
And in spite of my kicking and cursing
Under a ransom of kings he died.

I mourned that mule, and justly
Like the man who'd slain the goose
I led my wealth by a halter
And death had cut it loose.

Now, pockets filled from buckets,
Heavy with gold they feel,
Room for another quarter pound
Out with the flint and steel.

The nuggets sagged my pockets
And bounced my colt around
It broke my stride, I threw it aside
Pearl handled to the ground.

Too soon the last of my water
Measured for man, not a mule,
And the nuggets that weighted and fagged me
Made an ass as well as a fool.

But now my pockets are empty,
The map I've bargained away
To that glowering giant up in the sky
That controls the heat of the day.

The heat stampedes across this plain,
The sun keeps pressuring down
The searing, appalling dryness
Makes me feel like I could drown.

My lips are cracked my mouth is dry,
My eyes seem filled with sand
On my mother's grave, oh, why in Hell,
Did I come to this cursed land?

For nuggets of gold, of solid gold
That terrible useless lie,
That maid of the muck that lures a man
On to the desert to die.

But the gold is gone and I'm lightened
Not only just in weight,
I've lost a fortune in metal
But I've gained a fortune as great.

How great it is I might not find,
To know the foibles of men,
Unless I cross these miserable miles
And back to life again.

My lips are cracked, my mouth is dry,
My eyes seem filled with sand,
On my mother's grave, oh, why in hell,
Did I come to this cursed land?

For nuggets of gold, of solid gold
That terrible useless lie,
That siren of wealth that lures a man
On to the desert to die.

My lips are cracked, my mouth is dry,
My eyes seem filled with sand,
Nuggets of gold, of solid gold,
On to the desert to die…

Index

G

I

J

L

M

N

O

P

R

S

T

Printed in the United States
39312LVS00002B/337-369

9 781594 080678